THE LITTLE BOOK OF

MONEY

SPELLS

Other Books by Sophia

The Magical Garden
The Little Book of Office Spells
The Little Book of Love Spells
The Little Book of Hexes for Women

Sophia's Web Site:
www.psychicsophia.com

THE LITTLE BOOK OF
MONEY SPELLS

Sophia

**Andrews McMeel
Publishing**

Kansas City

01 02 03 04 05 RDS 10 9 8 7 6 5 4 3 2 1

Library of Congress Cataloging-in-Publication Data

Sophia, 1955–
The little book of money spells / Sophia.
    p. cm.
ISBN 0-7407-1422-8
    1. Magic. 2. Charms. 3. Finance, Personal—Miscellanea. I. Title.
BF1623.F55 S66 2001
133.4'4—dc21   00-049571

Book composition by Holly Camerlinck

To erma,
who taught me the real riches of life,
and
to James Sargent,
a golden boy who lived the life

Introduction

Money is energy. You can use it to power lots of things. This is the basic premise of this little book, because magic is also all about energy!

Money, like other forms of energy, is only good for what you can do with it. Money itself is just paper or, nowadays, numbers on a screen. For most of us, the goal is not money, but to acquire things we can *get* with money, right? So money is simply fuel for the engine of life, and magic is very similar. It is energy, but it is more direct; it can take any form to help you get what you want (if you know what you are doing). In this way we can view money as *material* magic.

So before you decide what this book can do for you, the first thing to do is sit down, relax, and think about this: What will make you happy? Money will not make you happy, but some of the stuff it will buy you will certainly do that! It's a trite saying, but it's true: Money does not buy happiness. Still, we all know that a *lack* of money brings certain misery. So the answer seems to be having the right amount for what you need to be content, right?

The universe is cool with helping you get what you need; it is even willing to indulge us as long as we don't get too greedy. But if you want money simply for the sake of wanting money, don't be surprised if you do not get it. If it is your Will to get some money for something, and it really is your True Will (what you are meant to do in this life), not an empty or TV-influenced semidesire, honey, you can get that money!

In this way money magic can help make you happy *unless* you get greedy, and as many legends tell us, the universe does not like that. Okay, I hear you mumbling about karma and deserving riches and getting all huffy because you think this means that the universe will only give you enough money for a small life—Wrongo! If you *need* those tiger-striped imported

Prada boots with platform heels, well then, you *need* them! It is all about attitude and honesty. The key? Will power, dahling!

So why isn't everyone rich? The answer to that is in two parts. The first is luck. Some are born into difficult circumstances for which they are not to blame. That is life and you do what you can. The second (and this probably applies to you if you have the money to buy this book) is that deep down many people simply do not feel that they deserve the prosperity that they should get in life. Why? Well, there are plenty of pop psych books and an army of therapists out there waiting to answer that question for you. We wouldn't want to compete with them, so we will just leave it as this: The things that limit you psychically and psychologically are all in your subconscious mind, and this is the place where all good spells work!

So am I saying this book is fun and therapeutic? Well, maybe! The point is, whether you call it magic, psychodrama, or hocus-pocus, if it works, why not use it, hm? And honey, this stuff works.

Here is an example and it is well documented.

I was on a local TV show here in my town promoting another one of my books and they asked me to show them a money spell. I then showed them the Magic Penny-Toss Spell (page 125). I mentioned that this spell was to get small amounts of quick cash—up to, say, a thousand dollars—for something you needed immediately. The next day someone phoned in and reported that she had done the spell because she really, really needed some cash, and within twelve hours she had won a scratch card for exactly a thousand dollars!

Why did the spell work for this housewife? Listen up and you will see the keys to money magic:

First, the woman who won really, really needed that cash, thus her desire was strong. Second, she got out there and bought some lottery tickets. In other words, she made an effort on her own to give the universe a chance to help her. Third, she followed the spell to the letter, with great verve and concentration—in other words, she put some energy into it! Fourth, she believed in it; willed belief is a key here!

Now, you may say she could have done all those things

minus the spell and won! Maybe yes, maybe no. That spell focused her power in a certain way, but—and this is important here—the power was *inside her*, it was *her* active willpower that got that spell to work!

And that is magic, my friend!

This is why I always say the magic is in you, and I never say that my spells will work for everyone, because if you don't have a spark, no engine is going to turn over!

Now, what about karma, you ask? Good question! Money is like any other form of energy: You hold on to it tightly, you horde it, you manipulate it for bad reasons, and it will kick back on you like an ornery mule! Notice that all the richest people in the world at some point suddenly start giving money away like mad? That's because deep down they know that their money karma is unbalanced. Never live for money, but use money to make your life fun and productive! Keep this in mind and live a balanced life. Be *generous* (especially if you do get a pile of moola), and be nice and play well with others, and you will do okay!

Okay, let's get to the good stuff! Here are my best money spells. Some are old, some are new, all of them can work—it's all up to you!

Coins, Cash, & Kisses,
Sophia

Penny-Finding Magic

An amazing number of children's rhymes hide some old spells and charms. Take this one, for example:

> "SEE A PENNY, PICK IT UP, ALL THE DAY
> YOU'LL HAVE GOOD LUCK."

This is actually based on a spell rooted in real folk magic. Finding a penny (once a real bit of money) means that money will come to you as well as good luck. This little charm marks the occasion with a real acknowledgment, that potential good luck can be made a reality. Here are some variations, some traditional, some not:

> SEE A PENNY, PICK IT UP, ALL THIS DAY I'LL HAVE
> GOOD LUCK!

If the head is facing you,
What you wish will soon come true!

If it is the back you see,
With your money go be free!

If a silver coin is found
All you invest will be sound.

If a coin is at your feet
Soon you will some money greet.

The following charms concern money found in different
places corresponding to the four elements:

Money found in earth
New profit will give birth

Money found in water
Gifts to son or daughter

Money found in air
Spend it without care!

Money found near fire
Grants your true desire!

GRAVEYARD SPELL FOR A FORTUNE

Okay, this is ghoulish, creepy, and weird—but it is traditional!
I include this for a bit of fun, though it probably isn't the most
enjoyable date activity for a Friday night.

YOU WILL NEED
+ A silver coin, or at least one that has silver on it,
like a dime, for example
+ A bit of courage!

THE SPELL
At midnight go to a graveyard and find the grave
of a very rich person. Leave a silver coin upon the grave,
saying three times:

I LEAVE A COIN UPON THIS GRAVE
SOON I WILL A FORTUNE SAVE!

Then thank the dead person. If you hear a strange sound, then the money will come, but if you are filled with terror, then the answer is no. Leave the coin and go.

Money Pie Spell

This is really more of a game than a serious money spell,
but after all, don't we all want that pie in the sky? Use this
when a few friends and you all need some fun money fast.
This is a way for everyone to join forces and get money for
the most needy! Anyway, brew a pot of tea and get down
with a pie in the sky!

You Will Need
+ All the makings for a fresh berry pie with the best
ingredients possible
+ A brand-new shiny penny

The Spell
Put the new penny in the fruit filling, saying:

BAKE A PENNY IN A PIE
TO US NOW GOOD LUCK WILL FLY!

Then bake it.

When ready to serve, everyone should touch the crust of the pie with a finger and close his or her eyes and think of what they need the money for.

Then, when you cut it to serve it, say this:

MONEY COME AND GO AROUND
MONEY COMES IF IT BE FOUND!

Whoever gets the penny in his piece should get money soon. Chew carefully, don't break a tooth! If it is not found right away, then money will come later. Keep the penny for good luck.

Tossing a Coin into Water for Luck

Who has not tossed a coin into a well or fountain and made a wish? Certainly not anyone who is reading *this* book! Wishing wells and sacred springs are very ancient magic, and making an offering to the spirit of such a place was said to definitely bring wealth, if you wished hard enough. Here are three traditional rhymes you can use to get what you wish for.

I throw a coin into a well
Soon my luck will grow and swell

Or

I offer a coin unto this spring
That unto me great wealth you'll bring

Or

I THROW A COIN INTO A CREEK
TO GET THE MONEY THAT I SEEK

Spring Tree Money Spell

"Money doesn't grow on trees, you know!"—or so my parents authoritatively let me know. Yet I have found, in a relative sense, that this isn't always true! Tree money magic is as old as the hills, and here is one such spell to try.

You Will Need
+ A small tree to plant (a birch, poplar, or oak is best)
+ A silver coin you have been carrying for at least a week

The Spell
On a full moon in the spring, plant the tree and put the coin among the roots of the tree, saying:

Here takes root the money tree
Each seed is gold, each leaf a bill

MAKING EASY ALL I SEE
EVERY NEED IT WILL FILL
AND SO IT IS
AND SO WILL BE
BY MOTHER EARTH
AND BY THIS TREE
JUSTICE AND CASH WILL BE
FOREVER HERE, FOREVER FREE!
HABONDIA!

Water this tree every day until it flourishes. Repeat the spell
every time you water it. Watch your finances grow as it grows!
Need a special favor? Talk to the tree (when no neighbors
are looking, of course!).

Home Prosperity Spells of the Four Directions

What should one do with all that loose change that seems to mysteriously appear in various places scattered about one's home? Use it in a money spell *for* your home! It was said that mysteriously appearing money was dropped by gnomes, and so was lucky! Save this lucky-found coinage in a small jar or cup until you are ready for this most excellent Home Prosperity Spell!

You Will Need
+ A small cup or jar of lucky coins you found

The Spell
When ready, in the early morning of a Sunday, do the following: Stand in the center of your home, close your eyes, and feel the

whole home. Then lean forward and shake the jar of coins like a rattle to each direction, saying the appropriate verse:

To the North:

IT GROWS FROM EACH DIRECTION
IT SCATTERS AT MY FEET
PROSPERITY AND CASH
IN THIS WORKING MEET
AHA!

To the South:

IT SHINES FROM EACH DIRECTION
IT SCATTERS AT MY FEET
PROSPERITY AND CASH
IN THIS WORKING MEET
AHA!

To the East:

IT FLIES FROM EACH DIRECTION
IT SCATTERS AT MY FEET
PROSPERITY AND CASH
IN THIS WORKING MEET
AHA!

To the West:

IT RAINS FROM EACH DIRECTION
IT SCATTERS AT MY FEET
PROSPERITY AND CASH
IN THIS WORKING MEET
AHA!

Then hold the jar over your head and say:

It comes from each direction
It scatters at my feet
It fills the coffers of my home
The work it may complete
Prosperity and cash
In this moment meet
Aha!

Afterward, randomly take some coins from the jar and hide one coin in every room. Tremendous luck and prosperity, it is said, will fill your home! Keep that jar of money somewhere and keep adding found coins to it. Every few months you can spend that money and start all over again!

Money for Good Works Spell

"They deserve more money!" I hear you cry, about your favorite nonprofit organization or charity. And you are so right! But instead of talking about it or donating a few bucks, why not put your magical mojo where your mouth is? It is said that this little spell can really help dump some needed cash into deserving hands!

You Will Need
+ Nine copper coins
+ A symbol on paper of what organization you wish the money for
+ A broom

THE SPELL

Assemble the coins and the paper item in a quiet room at sunset. Sweep around the room where you will do the spell, saying:

> CHASE AWAY THE TANGLES
> SWEEP AWAY THE NETS
> CHASE AWAY THE WRANGLES
> ALL INCREASE BEGETS!

Close your eyes and hold the coins in your hands. Shake them and chant:

> I AM THE MONEY SPIRIT
> I AM THE MONEY TREE
> FROM ME COMES ALL THE CASH
> AND ALL PROSPERITY
> HESTIA SO MOTE IT BE!

Let the coins cascade upon the paper symbol, and in your mind's eye see gold coins pour upon your favorite needy charity. Later, send or give those coins to that organization. They will be getting many more donations soon!

P.S. You can do this for deserving people as well!

Lakshmi

Lakshmi, the Hindu supreme goddess of prosperity, blessings, and power, has always been very, very good to me. Though honoring her is something that did not come from my family, I have always found that she comes through. The following blessing works especially well with businesses. Many Hindus have Lakshmi's image right near the cash register! There is a reason for this! Anyway, if you need long-term general cosmic mothering, Lakshmi is your Devi!

You Will Need

+ A stick of sandalwood incense
+ Matches
+ A little milk and honey (or spring water and honey if you're a vegan)
+ A beautiful cup

✦ An image of Lakshmi (easy to find)

THE SPELL

Do this alone on a full-moon night. Set up the image and, after cleaning the area, light the incense and mix the milk and honey together in the beautiful cup, saying:

OM SHRIM!

Sprinkle a drop of the milk-honey mixture to each direction and say:

GOLDEN MOTHER, BANISH HUNGER (EAST)
SHINING MOTHER, BANISH STRIFE (SOUTH)
COSMIC MOTHER, GIVE US PLENTY (WEST)
LOVING MOTHER, GIVE US LIFE (NORTH)

Place a drop on the center of the Lakshmi image, saying:

BLESSING GODDESS LAKSHMI
GRANT US
HEALTH, WEALTH, PROSPERITY, AND FREEDOM
LET POVERTY AND WANT BE BANISHED
BY YOUR FLOOD OF GOLD
SHRIM SVAHA!

Rub some of the mixture on the back of the image and "glue" it wherever she can do the most good, then say:

WE DRAW THE TREASURES OF THE EARTH
COME AND FILL, COME AND FILL
TO US WHO NEED WEALTH AND MIRTH
COME AND STAY, COME AND STAY
BE HERE ROOTED
NEVER FLY AWAY!
LAKSHMI !

Ta da! You have a real live goddess of wealth with you now! She is a great pal. Do some bonding and see what she brings *you!*

Lakshmi Water Pot Spell

"Oh no," I hear you say, "yet another Hindu spell invoking Lakshmi." Okay, I admit it! I'm a Lakshmi fan! To those who might be afraid this is gonna be a theme, this is the last one, so don't worry . . . but really, Lakshmi is a pal!

You Will Need
+ A small round ceramic pot with a lid
+ Natural pure water
+ Three silver coins

The Spell
Fill the pot with some water and put the coins in. Leave the jar open to the sun at midday, saying:

> GOLDEN MOTHER OF THE SUN
> BRIGHT AND PERFECT GODDESS
> SHINING FACE OF PLENTY, WARMTH, AND COMFORT
> FILL THIS VESSEL WITH YOUR GOLD
> FILL THIS CHALICE WITH YOUR ENERGY
> THAT I MAY PROSPER, THRIVE, AND GROW.

Later, cover the jar and leave it until the moon is out. A full moon is best, but at least it should be a waxing moon. Leave it open to the moon at midnight and say:

> MOTHER OF THE MOON
> GODDESS OF ALL ATTRACTION AND PLEASURE
> GREAT SILVER FACE OF PROSPERITY
> FILL THIS VESSEL WITH YOUR LOVE
> FILL THIS CHALICE WITH YOUR ENERGY
> THAT I MAY PROSPER, THRIVE, AND GROW.

Later, cover the jar and leave it until either sunset or sunrise.
Then bury the jar, covered and very carefully sealed, in a
special place. Say:

> Lakshmi, mother of the earth,
> Body of plenty, full and fleshed
> Green goddess
> Nourisher of all life and death
> Be here now by root and bud
> Fill this vessel with your green cash
> Fill this chalice with your energy
> That I may prosper, thrive, and grow.

Leave it for several days. Then unearth it at sunrise or sunset.
Now empty the water at the base of a tree and give each of
the coins to a friend. The money, it is said, will return a
thousandfold!

LEAP YEAR COIN SPELL

I swear this is a real old one, from the British side of my family. Don't ask me who I got it from, though!

An old English tradition tells us that you should collect coins marked with the dates of leap years in your kitchen. Keep them on a window ledge and every time you put one there, ask the elves to bring money to that house. One might say:

FAERIE FOLK NEVER SEEN
BRING US COINS FROM THE REALM BETWEEN!

For Money Protection

Some days just seem like baaaaaad money days, don't they? On
such days you might find yourself saying things like: "How did this
get here? How did all *that* money get spent? Who is playing who
in this financial transaction? Help! I need money mojo *now!*"

When you feel like money is slipping away or you are doing
business and you need protection and help, do this little spell:

You Will Need
+ A pin
+ A new one-dollar bill

The Spell

At midnight on a dark moon, prick your finger and, with the
blood, draw a five-pointed star, one point up, on the image of
the pyramid on the bill, then say:

POINT NOT AT ME
POINT NOW AWAY
STAR CHASES SHADOWS
AS NIGHT FLIES FROM DAY
THE WEALTH THAT I'VE GATHERED
WITH ME SHALL STAY!
ARADIA!

Carry it always. You can keep it in your wallet to protect you
from those out to get you!

Sword of Coins Big Money Charm

I love to travel and I am just hopelessly addicted to spells, so
when I find one I like, I sometimes wish to share it. This little
number is said to establish a great force for prosperity. *En garde!*

In China, swords formed of coins are very powerful magic
for attracting money. They combine symbols of wealth
and strong will!

You Will Need
+ Either a sword of coins you buy (try any Chinatown)
or one you make
+ Some rice wine (sake)

To make your own coin sword, glue coins to a red piece of
cardboard in the shape of a sword.

THE SPELL

Sprinkle the sword with the rice wine.
Wave your coin sword in a clockwise circle over your head
and say three times:

⊙M ZUN BA LA CHA LENG CHA NA YE SO HA!

It is traditional to hang it over one's bed or place of business,
always pointing from left to right.

New Moon Pocket-Turning Spell

Ever turn your pockets inside out to show a pal how broke
you were? If not, you probably don't need this book! Here is
an old spell based on the belief that the Lady Moon can bring
wealth to you—silver wealth in your pockets!

You Will Need
+ Nine silver coins
+ Two pockets to put them in

The Spell
When you first see the new crescent moon, take all
the coins out of your left pocket and show them to the moon.
Then say:

As you increase
So shall this money
As you get larger
So shall my wealth
The moon is in my pocket!

Then put the money in your right pocket and go home. Keep those coins in your pocket as long as you like, and as the moon grows, so shall your wealth!

Birthdate Coin Spell

Happy birthday to you! Happy birthday to you! Happy
birthday dear Gonna-have-money-luck-your-whole-life, happy
birthday to youuuuuuuuu! This here is an old charm that
is said to grant good money luck for a lifetime!
One can only hope . . .

You Will Need
+ A coin that was issued on your birth year—a silver dollar
is best and most traditional

The Spell
Hold this coin to your heart and say:

As we have a common birth
Bring me riches, joy, and mirth!

Keep it with you always—don't ever spend it!

This is also a very, very cool magical gift to give a
newborn baby!

New Year's Money Spell

"May old accountants be forgot and . . . and . . ."—shoot! I can't remember the rest! Well, anyway, we all know that New Year's Day has special magic. In some countries, like Japan, it is the biggest festival of the year! Here in the West, New Year's used to have more powerful meaning, the message of which was "starting anew," something we can all use now and then, right? Try this spell and see if you can't get the New Year off on the right foot.

You Will Need
+ Two new silver coins
+ New socks and new shoes to wear on New Year's Eve
+ A pair of old shoes you keep in the closet

THE SPELL

On New Year's Eve, place a silver coin in each new shoe before you put it on. Keep the coins there all night long. Make sure that you dance at least one dance and kiss someone at least once!

As the New Year tolls, close your eyes and see yourself showered with silver coins for the New Year.

If you do this, money will follow you and your earnings will increase all that year. Keep the coins in a pair of old shoes in your closet all year long.

Mention Me in Your Will

Do you have a family member that has one foot in the grave
and the other on a banana peel? Before they go to the other
side, wouldn't it be great if they mentioned you in their will?
And you are *so* deserving! After all, "you can't take it with
you." Might as well leave it to a relative that can use it . . .
like *you!*

You Will Need
+ Access to the family plot in a cemetery
+ Five nickels
+ A photograph of you and the family member in question
(if you do not have one of the two of you together,
use Photoshop or some tape)

THE SPELL

At midday, go to a cemetery and take some loose dirt from your family plot. Lay five nickels near any relative's tombstone. Say the following invocation:

OH —— (NAME AND RELATIONSHIP, E.G., "UNCLE BOB")

OF YOU I AM FOND
LEAVE ME WEALTH
FROM THE BEYOND
IF YOU LOVE ME
DO AS I SAY
BY THE POWER
OF HECATE!

Leave the coins in the dirt and take some of the earth home with you. Scatter it about your home, repeating the charm. Rub a bit on the photo.

Say the charm one last time and send the photo to your
elderly relative with a kind note.
It may be a little ghoulish to be a pregrave robber, but hey,
they won't need the money where they are going!

(Note: Hecate is pronounced HEH-ka-teh.)

☉Ur Lady of Overspending Spell

Some of us just tend to overdo it at times. Or is that *overdue* it? You are trying to do better, you would really rather save your money for that vacation in Paris, but then you spy that little something that is just perfect and . . . You need a spell to get some financial control! To rein in those spending flings, you need a heap of juju protection and a prayer to Our Lady of Overspending! By the way, you can do this for others (a son, daughter, or spendthrift friend) as well!

You Will Need
+ A body of water (if you are not near any lakes, rivers, or oceans, then a bathtub is fine)
+ Matches
+ One white votive candle

✦ A bit of lavender
✦ A seashell

The Spell
On a Monday at evening, go to the body of water, light the candle, and say:

LADY OF WATERS
LADY OF PEACE
BANISH ALL PROBLEMS
GRANT US RELEASE!
MA-RE, MA-RE, MA-RE!

Then place the lavender in the shell, pour a little water into the shell over the lavender, put the shell near the water, and say:

LADY OF CALM
LADY OF BLUE
KEEP ONE FOCUSED

KEEP ONE TRUE
MONEY SAVE
MONEY EARN
MONEY LOST
NOW RETURN!
MA-RE!

Pour the contents of the shell into the water and blow out the candle and bury it. Dry the shell (don't wash it!) and keep it on your desk at home or in your office. Or give it as a present to a spendthrift who needs restraint. You will find that a whole lot less money is going out, and that means more will stay!

Remove a Money Hex

Maybe you have been cursed, or maybe your karma just simply ran over your dogma *and* the rent is due! Strings of bad luck can seem, well, a little suspicious at times. If you feel like you're jinxed in the money department, that cash seems to avoid you or disappear when you appear, this traditional little spell will unhex you and clear the cosmic air so you can get what you earned!

You Will Need
+ A willow tree near running or clear water
+ Paper money, of whatever denomination you need to use (If you feel the hex is minor, then a dollar; if you feel it is major, a larger bill is called for—it depends on the amount of mojo you want to put into it)

THE SPELL

At midnight, when the moon is completely dark, go to the willow and lean against the trunk, saying:

LADY OF THE DARKENING MOON
HEAR MY SPELL
HEAR MY RUNE
UNCHAIN MY WEALTH
UNHEX ME SOON!

Close your eyes and breathe deeply, see the bad energy being absorbed by the willow, feel the green energy enter you. When you feel cleansed, roll up the bill and tie it up with a thin hanging branch of the tree. Say:

BANE BE GONE
SO MOTE IT BE
IO EVOEE
IAI-MA!

43

Leave and never return to that tree again. Things will begin to improve, and by full moon you should be better!

Money-Laundering Spell

No, no, no—it's not what you think! You don't need an offshore account in the Bahamas or a shady business to do this spell. This ancient spell from Asia calls more money into your home through washing cash. At least your money will be sanitary and, hey, Martha Stewart would love it! Seriously, this is an old one many swear by.

You Will Need
+ A natural spring (you could cheat and use bottled spring water, if you must!)
+ All the money you can find in the house at the time you decide to do the spell
+ A sieve of some kind
+ A piece of white unused cloth

THE SPELL

At noon on a sunny day, go to the spring when you can be pretty much alone and place the money in the sieve, saying:

INCREASE, INCREASE
MONEY I EARN

Wash the money with water from the spring, saying:

KUBERA, KUBERA
TURN MONEY TURN

Shake it dry, saying:

RAIN FROM THE SKY
YEARN MONEY YEARN

Wrap it in the white cloth, saying:

WHAT I YEARN
TURN
WHAT I EARN
RETURN!
HAMSA!

Keep the money in a jar, a piggy bank, or some kind of neat container. It is said that more money will flow to you day after day if you keep this. At the end of the year, spend all the money in the cloth and do it all over again!

Give Me Money, Honey!

Sunlight, honey, bees, pollen, gold, warm days . . . ah! All
these summery images taste of prosperity and wealth, don't
they? That's why you call your lover honey, right? We could
call this the "fund-raising/networking spell." This spell is great
for parties or special dinners or barbecues where you are
collecting money, networking, or fund-raising. Add a little
magic honey to the scene and watch the gold fly!

You Will Need
+ A sunny warm day and a bright, hidden spot filled
with sunlight where you can set the jar for a time
+ A jar of pure honey (wildflower is best)
+ A well-cleaned gold coin or other gold item

THE SPELL

On a Sunday at noon, when the sun is shining, take the gold
item and jar outside. Drip a bit of the honey on the ground
and taste it, saying:

SALVE APIA
JOY TO THEE
SOL INVINCUS
GOLD OF THE BEE!

Drop the clean gold item into the honey and close the lid.
Hold it up to the sun and say:

MIDAS TOUCH
TRANSFORMS TO GOLD
SWEETEN THE GIVING
OF YOUNG AND OLD!
SOL INVINCUS!

Leave the jar in the sun for one hour exactly, then bring it in.

Take the gold item out of the honey and wash it. Then use the honey in preparing food to feed the whole party. The honey could be added to lemonade or barbecue sauce, it doesn't matter, just as long as all those potential donors or clients get a taste! Also, wear the gold item during that party.

Honey, those guests will be throwing money at you by the time you are done, or maybe networking business offers. There are all kinds of honey, and they are all sweet!

Pot o' Gold at the End of the Rainbow Spell

Still believe in magical money and buried treasure? Sure you do! Why else would you be reading a book like this? The old myth that a pot of gold lies under the end of a rainbow has some ancient roots. The rainbow has always been a lucky sign and one that means prosperity. This little spell will help you capture a bit of this rainbow luck in your own pot o' gold—who knows what buried treasure you may find?

You Will Need
+ A small pot with a lid (pottery is best)
+ A clear bit of glass or a crystal
+ A rainbow!

THE SPELL

Keep your little pot with the crystal or glass piece inside it
handy. When you see a rainbow forming, take the pot outside
quickly and remove the top. Tilt it so that the rainbow is
reflected in the glass or crystal and say:

RAINBOW BRIGHT
I GATHER THEE IN
RAINBOW LIGHT
REVEAL WHAT'S WITHIN
SECRET TREASURES
REVEAL TO MY EYE
SPIRITS OF WEALTH
I PULL FROM THE SKY!
EOS IRIS!

When the rainbow begins to fade, quickly cover the pot and
bring it inside.

That night, at midnight, sit in a dark room facing east. Slowly open the pot and stare into the dark depths, saying:

Iris, open my eyes
That I may see
Secret treasures
Waiting for me!

You'll see some rainbow colors and then a strange vision of where some secret wealth might be hiding. One friend had a vision of some things from her attic that turned out to be valuable antiques, so keep that third eye *and* your mind open!

CHARM FOR ASKING
THE WEE PEOPLE FOR HELP

Do you believe in faeries? Elves? Little people that run around
dancing in the moonlight, playing tricks on humans? Fairy
tales, right? Well, some people seriously believe that nature
spirits like elves and leprechauns can help poor but kindly
folk when they are strapped for money. It is doubtful that the
wee folk will lead you to buried gold (how many people bury
gold anymore?), but you never know! Give this ancient charm
a try and see what happens!

You Will Need
+ A lovely stone
+ A blooming foxglove plant or a natural hole
in any kind of tree
+ A piece of cake and a small thimble of milk

THE SPELL

On a full-moon night, place the stone at the foot of the blooming foxglove (or in the hole of the tree) and place the piece of cake and small vessel of milk on the stone, saying:

TUATHA DE DANNAN
By MIDNIGHT AND NOON
I CALL TO THE SIDHE
TO GRANT ME A BOON.

Whisper into the foxglove (or tree hole) your monetary desires—plead your case for deserving what you want, it is okay to flatter faeries! Mention the cake and such—lay it on thick! When done, turn to depart and say:

THANKS TO THE WEE FOLK
By NOON AND MIDNIGHT
GIFTS OF SIDHE
BLESS DAY AND NIGHT!

Odd coincidences, good luck, lucky finds, and mischievous boons will soon dance through your life. Once called, the wee folk are said to continue the relationship if they like you. A bit of food and drink once in a while are considered neighborly, but be warned, they do like to play tricks!

HOT MONEY SPELL

Eros and money, how the words roll off the tongue, right? The two always seem to be close to the root of most pleasure and pain. Lots of spells mention that you can often get one with the other! This is a way to use your erotic energy to get money. Use it if you dare, but remember: You really *are* playing with fire! Sizzzzzzzle!

YOU WILL NEED
+ Some rose oil or scent
+ A five-dollar bill
+ Matches

THE SPELL
Before going to bed on a Friday night, place some rose scent on the bill and on your forehead, heart, and lower belly area, saying:

Action, knowledge, will
Sun, moon, and fire
Come together now
Grant my desire
Om shakti-kama!

Place the bill in your underpants or jammies pants, you know
where, then go to bed and have erotic fantasies about what
you will do with your new money . . . then fall asleep.

The next day, burn the bill when you awake and rub some of
the ashes on your body, then says this:

Om svaha
Shakti svaha
Kama svaha!

Be careful what you wish for, you just might get it! Ignition on!
Sparks will fly and who can say what will happen when the
erotic and money collide!

Savings Spell

Everyone says we should save for a rainy day, but money just slips through our fingers. How can so much cash flit away and so little end up being saved? Well, obviously *you* have to save the money, but this traditional spell is said to get the savings vibe going and keep sudden expenses at bay—why not "tie one on" and see for yourself?

You Will Need
+ Matches
+ A small white candle
+ A bank book, piggy bank, bank card, or some other symbol of savings for you
+ Some red cotton thread

THE SPELL

When the moon is just showing a crescent (waxing), on a
Saturday night, light the candle and walk three times around
the assembled items, saying:

> HOLD BY NIGHT
> HOLD BY THE LIGHT
> HOLD HOLD HOLD
> BY CANDLE WHITE
> ADHERE EST!

Pass your piggy bank, passbook, or bank card over the flame
three times, saying:

> HOLD ON TO WHAT'S DEAR
> BY THE FLAME SO BRIGHT!

Wrap the red thread slowly three times about the piggy bank
or about the first page of the passbook or card, saying:

THREE TIMES ABOUT
THREE TIMES I BIND
HOLD AND INCREASE
LUCK BE KIND
FOREVER TO SAVE
WILL BE ON MY MIND
THREE TIMES ABOUT
THREE TIMES I BIND

Tie the thread off. Then blow out the candle.

Keep the red thread on the item if possible. If not, gently pull it off without breaking it and keep it in your wallet . . . and watch those pennies! The universe will try to help, but in the end it's up to you!

BEST EVER CREDIT-CARD
PROTECTION SPELL

Okay, this one is not exactly handed down from my great-grandmother. She did not know what plastic was, but she sure would have loved it if she had, trust me! Though c-cards are fairly new, credit is not, and this little spell (though mutated just a tad) has roots firmly in the "it's my money and I don't want no one touching it" tradition of the ancients. All that and it's easy, too! So take the time and put a mojo on your Visa (or AmEx or MasterCard) and protect it from evil, both human . . . and others!

YOU WILL NEED
+ Your credit card
+ Some salt
+ One fresh sage leaf

THE SPELL

At midnight on a Tuesday, lay the card faceup on a clean table
with low light on in the room (candles are always nicer)

Touch the card and say:

Mine is mine
FOREVER AND A DAY
HERE IT IS GATHERED,
HERE IT WILL STAY!

Draw a circle of salt about the card, saying:

AVERT AND AWAY
ALL EVIL AND THEFT
FLY OUT AS SHADOWS
NONE BE BEREFT!

Rub the card with the sage leaf in clockwise circles ten times.

As you do so, in your mind's eye see the card being wrapped in a protective green ring of light, then say:

ABOUT THE LIGHT
WRAPS IT TIGHT
EVIL TAKES FLIGHT
THE TRIUMPH OF RIGHT!
MALUS AVERTUS!

When done, scoop up the salt and wash it away in water. Let the leaf dry and burn it. Pocket the card and know that no one should ever be able to use it against you. Of course, you might still max it out, but then, that is your problem!

Excellent Higher-Yield Investment Spell

Okay, maybe you missed out on the last big stock split and you didn't buy shares in that cyber company that went through the roof and you ignored that last tip that made your local hairdresser wealthy, *but* now you are ready to make your move! You are buying the dot-com stocks, or bonds you *know* will grow, grow, grow, or maybe you are investing in a startup? The point is, it's a gamble and you want it to blossom and skyrocket! This little spell will light the fuse and send it soaring!

You Will Need
+ A drinking cup with some moistened potting soil in it
+ One of the bonds or stocks (or a copy of same) that is to be influenced

* Matches
* A stick of pine or cedar incense
* Three beans (fertile)

THE SPELL

On the first day that the new crescent moon can be seen, a short time after sunset, place the cup of earth on top of the document representing your investment. Light the incense and point it to each of the four directions. Each time, say:

OUT TO THE QUARTER
UP TO THE HEIGHT
FULL OF POWER
FULL OF MIGHT
HADITH!

Finally, stick the incense in the cup. Being careful not to knock the incense over, plant the three beans in the wet earth, saying:

CENTERED AND STRONG
GROW WITH THIS LIFE
PROSPEROUS AND LONG
SKY FATHER, EARTH WIFE!
BEL ERDA LET IT BE!
GROW TALL AND GROW FREE!

Let the incense burn down completely and keep the planted
beans watered until they sprout.

Repeat the last verse every day when you water it,
if you have time.

As the beans germinate and sprout, so too, it is said, will your
investment grow. You can plant them outside when they are
really growing and you can begin the process all over again.
Now we know that whoever said "that doesn't mean beans"
didn't know what they were talking about!

Ᾱest Egg Spell

This works best in the springtime and should be done to get a steady income from an investment or a piece of property you've just bought. This could also be called the "one in the hand is worth two in the bush" spell, but of course you don't want all of your eggs in one basket (or spell)!

You Will Ᾱeed
+ A small, healthy, flowering bush (some good money-attracting bushes to use are rhododendron, forsythia, juniper, or myrtle)
+ A place to plant it
+ A shovel
+ Three silver coins

+ A paper with some kind of representation
of your investment (maybe even a picture)
+ A cup of fresh spring water

THE SPELL

Find a good spot for your bush and make sure that it is safe as well. A big pot is fine too. No matter what, you don't want it cut down, right? Talk about your negative juju!

Close your eyes and silently chat with the bush. Ask it to bring you prosperity and in return you will take care of it. If you feel good vibes from the bush, go on; if not, then give this one to a friend and get a new one!

Now, on a nice day when the moon is waxing, bring everything to the spot you have chosen and dig a hole.

Toss in the three coins and say:

> SILVER COME, SILVER GO
> SILVER COME, HERE NOW FLOW!

Place the paper/image of your spell-desire in the hole and say:

> PLANTED NOW IN SOLID EARTH
> GROW AND GROW AND GROW IN WORTH!

Plant the bush, quietly asking it for help, then water it with your special water and say:

> FLOW IN EARTH—GROW IN WORTH
> BUSH AND SILVER WEAVE FOR ME
> GROWTH AND WEALTH: PROSPERITY!

Now, to really make sure this spell works you need to water it every evening for seven days and whisper the final verse to it as you do so.

Over the months and years, treat the bush as a friend. Keep it healthy and water and feed it, especially when your investment needs a little help or when you add to it!

Teatime Mental Money Magic Meditation

It is easy to forget that money is just an idea, just like other
ideas. It comes and goes, fills out minds, and then slips away.
The people who make real money usually do so from ideas
and work, with some will thrown in. Often we become so
fixated or anxiety ridden about money that we psychically
push it away! If you are in a money quandary, thinking about
a new job, or just brainstorming about ways of getting cash,
this meditation will help you tremendously. Not exactly a
money spell, this money meditation will open your mind so
you can receive inspiration and inner guidance. Take a pause
so that the universe can give you what you want. Kick back
and relax, things are about to get better!

You Will Need

+ Some spring water
+ A pot to boil it in that is not steel or aluminum
+ Matches
+ Some dried basil
+ Some fresh mint (fresh if possible, but dried is okay)
+ A small ceramic or glass teapot

The Meditation

On an appropriate Monday, in the morning if possible, boil the water and burn a little of the dried basil as incense, saying:

> Clear the air
> Of all strife
> Health and wealth
> Come into my life!

When the water boils, add it to the teapot that is filled with three leaves (or pinches) of basil and quite a bit of mint. Say:

WYRD SISTER THREE
AS HERBS YOU BE
LET ME SEE
PROSPERITY!

As it steeps, smell the steam and open your mind. Let all your cares float away with the scent, relax all your muscles, and close your eyes. Think of nothing at all.

Then pour a cup of tea for yourself or for you and your friends (if you are doing this with a group), and say:

I CONJURE WEALTH
AS INSPIRATION
I CONJURE WEALTH
WITH IMAGINATION
I CONJURE WEALTH
BY CLEAR CREATION!

Now, sip your tea and let your thoughts flow. Write down all good ideas, doodle, be silly, have fun, let it flow, and be open and creative. Do not focus on your problems or on your stress. Take a mental vacation! Silence!

When the tea is completely gone, bury the tea leaves outside and say:

Wyrd sisters three
I thank thee
Let me now make
The most of me!

Later, go back through your ideas and notes—you will find some gems there. Not just money or job ideas, but ways to make yourself happier! And isn't that *really* what it is all about?

Cash Register Charm

If you own a small business, and it seems like everyone does today, you need to keep that cash flow coming! This charm will work equally well for a cash register or a tip jar. Keep that money flowing in, right now!

You Will Need
+ A small magnet, any kind as long as it is small
+ A piece of fresh rosemary
+ A hundred-dollar bill

The Charm
On the day of a full moon, in the early morning, take the magnet and the rosemary sprig. Rub the sprig into the magnet until it falls to pieces, saying:

> FREYA GREEN
> BOUNTY CHARM
> MAKE THIS BRIGHT
> MAKE THIS WARM
> LIKE BEES TO ROSEMARY
> MONEY SWARM!

Let the pieces of rosemary fall to the ground, then wrap the magnet in the hundred-dollar bill, saying:

> LOADSTONE LISTEN
> LOADSTONE HEAR
> FEEL THIS MONEY
> WE HOLD DEAR
> SEEK IT OUT
> BRING IT NEAR!

Keep this charm in your till (or tip jar!) for three days. Then go ahead and spend that hundred dollars on something you need with no debating or discussing. From that time on, keep the magnet in with other cash—never leave it bare! It should always have some money, even just a dollar, on top of it. If things are slow, rub the magnet and repeat the final verse and business will pick up!

Money Guardian Spell

Don't quite trust your bank's vault? Think your safe may not be so? Keep cash in a drawer and are a bit uneasy? You need your own private security guard, though one who doesn't ask for pay or breaks or a 401(k) plan, right? Well, I have a little doll magic for you . . . and it is guaranteed to make any thief think twice and maybe have a nightmare or two!

You Will Need
+ A very small doll, either made by you or bought
+ Some red thread

The Spell
On the dark of the moon, at midnight, sit quietly and empty your mind. Concentrate on how your money needs protecting. Take the doll and wash it carefully, saying:

> Shout shout
> Inside and about
> Guardian come in
> All evil stay out!

Dry it off and look at it. Breathe on it three times, saying:

> Shabti!
> By my breath
> By the air
> Guard my money
> From all who dare.

Rub your index finger on its heart, saying:

> Shabti!
> By my skin
> By my need
> Guard my money
> From all greed.

Take one hair from your head and bind it to the doll
with red thread, saying:

> SHABTI!
> BY MY HAIR
> A BINDING I MAKE
> GUARD MY MONEY
> FROM ALL WHO TAKE.

Kiss the doll, saying:

> SHABTI!
> BY MY KISS
> AND ALL I FEEL
> GUARD MY MONEY
> FROM ALL WHO STEAL!

Then hold it tight to your heart, saying:

АПКН SHABTI HA!

Now you have a little servant who will protect your money, whether it is in a safety-deposit box, a safe, a drawer, or a briefcase. It will be effective for up to a year; then, if you want it to keep working for you, you must do the ritual again. And never let anyone tell you that grown-ups shouldn't play with dolls!

Pay Me Back Spell

Paybacks can be a witch, or so they say, especially if it is a friend who owes you money. Or maybe it is less personal and more serious, like a big amount is owed you? Oh no! The check is in the mail? Baloney! But you can help make it so! Not only will this spell help you get your moola back, you might get interest as well!

You Will Need
+ A small piece of gray paper
+ A purple pen
+ Matches
+ A yellow candle
+ One of the debtor's business cards (or something relating to the debtor)

The Spell

On the next dark moon, take out the piece of gray paper and, with the purple pen, write how much the debtor owes you and this rune, saying:

You owe me
I hold no hate
Give me my money
Before it's too late

Then light the candle, placing it on top of the business card and the gray paper, saying:

Hear my roar and hear my plea
Give my money back to me
As I will so may it be
Svaha!

Burn the gray paper. Leave the business card
under the candle.

Let the candle burn down (in a holder, of course!). When it is
done, if this is possible, send the debtor back his or her
business card with a note saying how much he or she owes,
then wait for that cash to come flying back!

Look Like Your Family Has Money Spell

"You look like a million!" Doesn't everyone live to hear that? Know what it *really* means? It means that you've got the "rich vibe"—you look wealthy! Looking wealthy is almost as good as being wealthy. Ever hear about those folks who keep crashing jet-set parties even though they are nobodies? They've got the aura, and we know rich attracts rich, right?

Use this little spell to cast a glamour and project the feeling of high society that you want to be in. This spell will help you get the seal of approval from the well-to-do and no one will be the wiser.

You Will Need
+ Mirror

+ Matches
+ A light blue candle
+ A small piece of malachite
+ Some expensive perfume (or cologne for men)
+ Some real family jewelry
+ Some classy clothes

THE SPELL
Set up everything in front of the mirror.
Light the candle, saying:

ALL IS NOT
WHAT IT MAY SEEM
IN FAERIE LIGHT
I WEAVE MY DREAM!

Place the malachite piece into the perfume bottle,
close it, and shake it, saying:

> FAERIE OF GLAMOURS
> BLESS MY INTENT
> CHANGE LEAD TO GOLD
> EMPOWER THIS SCENT!

Anoint your body with the scent and also pick up the jewelry.
Place the jewelry next to your heart and say:

> MY RAGS BECOME RICH
> I BECOME ROYALTY
> FROM COMMONER I SWITCH
> FOR ALL HIGHBORN TO SEE!

Put on the jewelry and get dressed. Continue to stare at yourself
in the mirror, seeing a rich aristocratic princess or prince.

When done, get ready to go out and say:

May all my dreams
Through glamour come true
May others believe
That my blood is blue!

Kiss your reflection in the mirror, blow out the candle, and go out and knock them dead! Grrrrrrr! Go get 'em, tiger!

Mad Money Spell

Okay, you don't *really* need a chunk of cash now,
but you have (choose one) :

Broken up with a lover
just had a great defeat
just had a great victory
have PMS like a bear
uhhhhh . . . well, you just need to *shop!*

Anyway, you want—no, *need*—to go blow money on
something frivolous and unnecessary—come on, be honest,
just to lift your spirits! Maybe you are being called out with a
mad shopping posse of fellow consumer-hungry friends. But
you need a piece of cash to fall into your lap to do this! Here
is a spell for this very thing—cash for *fun*—but the catch is

this: If you get the money, you have to blow it in a silly manner or you won't get such a blessing again! Banks are for wimps—go spend!

You Will Need
+ A few minutes near the entrance of a park or yard
+ A new dollar bill
+ A red marker

The Spell
On a chosen Friday at twilight, go to the entrance of the park or yard and take out the new dollar. Rub it on your forehead, saying:

I know I know
I need money to blow
Bala- ma
Om ha!

Rub it on your chest, saying:

I FEEL I FEEL
MAKE CASH REAL
SHAKTI-MA
OM HA!

Rub it discreetly on your groin area, saying:

I NEED I NEED
FEED MY GREED
LILA- MA
OM HA!

Take your pen and draw a big X (the rune for "gift") on it and imagine the cash falling upon your head like snow.

Then rip the bill into a million little pieces and throw them into the air above you with giggles and wild abandon! Throw open your arms with your eyes closed and feel a great money pile descend—come to Mama!

When that mad money comes—fairly soon, I might add—spend it very quickly! The Wild Powers want these wild urges to be fun and spontaneous. Too much thinking shorts out this magic! Yippie!

Spring Free Money Spell

Okay, you have this money, but, well, you really don't . . . your cash might be tied up in a trust or in some sort of weird contractual hold or in a bank CD or part of an unreleased settlement or . . . you get the idea. It is yours, you need it, you have it—but you really don't! This is a spell that will open up that door, break down that wall, pry open those fingers and/or light a fire under that bureaucrat's buttkis—or, well, whatever needs to happen to spring that cash!

You Will Need
+ A small inexpensive wooden box
+ A brown marker pen
+ Five one-dollar bills
+ A smooth rock (fist size or a bit larger) from a stream bed or beach if possible

THE SPELL

On the night before a new moon, at midnight, take the box
and write upon it with the marker pen the exact
thing that is holding the money you want
(example: GRANDPA SMITH'S "&%$#" TRUST FUND).

Next, stack the five dollar bills and fold them in half. Fold
them in half again, and in half yet again. Say each time:

> MONEY BOUND
> ROOTED TO GROUND
> HERE NOW FOUND!

Put the wad of cash into the wooden box and bury it in some
dirt (anywhere is fine). Put the rock on top and remain
completely silent, focusing on the bondage your money is in
and your frustration. Walk away in silence.

The next day, as the moon becomes new, just after midnight, dig the box up, take the rock, and smash the box while yelling:

Money spring free
Io evoee!

Pull the money out of the smashed box, unfold it, then wave all the free bills above you, saying:

Money now free
Fly now to me
So may it be!

Keep those five bills in your wallet. Do not spend them! Bury the pieces of the box in the dirt and toss the rock. Then sit back, sip a cool one, and wait for the barriers to fall! When that cash is sprung, go spend the magic bills in your wallet right away.

Money Hunch Spell

Most people who make money on the stock market or in other risky professions seem to have a sixth sense, don't they? They may be clueless on how to write a decent sentence (horrors!), but somehow they know when to gamble and when to stop. How can one develop this money sense? Well, we will admit that some of this is born talent, but this spell will tickle that intuition and help you to get in touch with those inspirational money hunches. Whether it is deciding about stocks, contracts, business opportunities, or simply which car is the best to buy, trust that inner voice. Try this spell to hear it loud and clear!

You Will Need
+ Matches
+ A stalk of dried lavender

> ✦ An ashtray or other dish
> ✦ A feather
> ✦ A pad of paper and a pen

THE SPELL

On a Wednesday morning, sit comfortably where you usually make money decisions and breathe deeply. Light the dry lavender flower with a match and place it smoking into the ashtray. Fan the smoke onto your head, saying:

CLARITY CLARITA
PUTO EST SENTENTIA
INNER GENIUS—MAY I KNOW
HOW TO MAKE MY MONEY GROW
CURO ET FAVEO!

Touch the feather to your closed eyes and forehead and open your mind. You may ask any question. (Example: "How should I invest this money?")

With your eyes half open and completely relaxed, hold the feather in one hand, hold the pen in the other, and doodle on the pad, draw or write down anything that comes to mind, no matter how silly.

When done, simply put the feather down. And say:

FAVEO—SO I SEE
INNER GENIUS, GROW IN ME!
THANK YOU FOR THE CLARITY!

You will find a hint of the answer to your question in your doodles. You can do this spell a lot to develop your hunch-sense, if you like. The more you do this, the more your inner money sense will grow. Always use the same feather and it will become a powerful insight charm for you!

Never abuse the power of this spell! (Well, a few horse races and card games are okay, but that's all!)

Employer Payback Spell

They promised a quick raise, you got nada. Overtime? Sorry! Perks? Soon, really! And they deducted *what* from your paycheck? Yow! Employers have a thousand ways they can mess with your money. Make 'em pay up and play fair with this little spell. Unions are good, but magic is sometimes better!

You Will Need
+ A self-made typed or written "receipt"
saying what is owed you
+ A red pen
+ A bit of sage

The Spell
On a Tuesday at midnight, do this spell at a window,
looking south.

Take the receipt and sign the name of the employer who owes you at the bottom, in red. See that person in your mind giving you the money. Get mad! Wrap the receipt about the sage and twist it, saying:

Ringio, rangio
To me
To me
To me you owe
Pay you fair
Pay you nigh
Thou payest me
By and by!
Rangio, ringio
So it come, let it go!

Open the window and call the money to you. Burn the paper with sage, saying:

High thee hence
Over the hill
Over the fence
It is my will
Ringio rangio
Make it so!

Let the ashes fall out the window and leave it open the rest of the night. If that money doesn't come within a week, send or give some sage to your boss for memory, after repeating the last verse. You'll get your moola from the cheap SOBs—then look for a new job!

Fruit of Prosperity Spell

Sometimes your life gets into a funk, money seems to simply avoid you, and a dark cloud hovers over your life. The vibe of prosperity and "all is well" seems absent! You need to bring it back into the house or apartment and plunk it down on the kitchen table and say, "I am one happy son of a gun and things are gonna go *good* for me." This is a quick stop-by-the-grocery-store spell that will do the trick. It works great for down-in-the-dumps pals as well!

You Will Need
+ A pineapple, a coconut, or a pomegranate
+ Some rosewater
+ A glass or ceramic bowl

SOPHIA   3/17/0~ - Fruit to
eaten on
24th

THE SPELL
On a <u>sunny Sunday</u>, around <u>noon</u>, take your lovely, perfect
fruit and hold it up to the sun and then to the four directions,
saying each time:

Io POMONA!
PROSPERITY!
CORNUCOPIA
SO MAY IT BE!

Sprinkle a bit of rosewater on it, saying:

POMONA DEA
HERE THOU ARE
ALIGHT FROM AFAR
CORNUCOPIA YOU GIVE
WELL WE WILL LIVE!
IO POMONA!

104

Place the fruit in a nice clean ceramic or glass bowl in the center of your kitchen table (or on a friend's kitchen table). Then take the rosewater and sprinkle it all over—well—everything in the house!

It is important that the fruit be eaten with joyous gusto no later than one week after it is blessed, and it can then be replaced with yet another blessed fruit. This spell also adds that extra zap to fruit gift baskets! Here is a new magical diet: eating your way to prosperity!

Keep That Wallet Full Spell

Nothing is worse than reaching for your wallet after getting
rung up and suddenly realizing (*boing!*) that you are out of
cash . . . you fool! Okay, plastic saves us all at times, but how
embarrassing! And where does that cash go, anyway? Well,
unless you live with a wallet mooch (if you do, there is no
hope), this little spell will help keep your wallet full and ping
your psyche when you need to replenish.

You Will Need
+ A large, perfect bay leaf
+ An orange marker or pen

The Spell
On a Wednesday, in the early morning, when the moon is
waning, take up the bay leaf. Turn about three times clockwise

and draw this image with the marker on one side
of the leaf, saying:

MONEY LIGHT
MONEY FREE
GREEN LIT LEAVES
OF THE MONEY TREE
AS YOU FALL
RETURN TO ME
CRUMENS SERVO
SO IT BE!

Place the leaf into your billfold, in a place where it will be
safe. It must not crack or break; if it does, make a new one!

And remember! Never leaf your wallet lying around! Someone
might rake it!

Grant Me This Money!
(A Spell to Get Fellowships, Grants, and Scholarships)

You need money for a special goal and you may be thinking, "I'm more deserving than others because I need money for a very important project or for my crucial education. So I deserve—I repeat, *deserve*—to get money for it from someone who has too much to begin with!" There are a lot of money giveaways out there, but there's also a lot of competition. So focus your will, get those forms, and apply, apply, apply! And just to stack the deck in your favor, here is a spell!

You Will Need
+ A copy of the grant, fellowship, or other thing you are applying for
+ Matches

+ Some dried crumbled oak leaf and dried
  pine needles mixed together
  + A small dish to burn them in

The Spell
On a full moon, face east, touch the forms, and clap your
hands three times. Then say:

> Mind and hand
> Word and deed
> True will planned
> Bring money I need!

Light the leaf and pine needle mixture and swirl the
application and/or papers through the smoke three times, in a
spiral motion, clockwise, saying:

> Spiral of mind
> Spiral of need

MERCURIUS BIND
MY WORD NOW HEED!
PHOS!

Visualize your papers filled with light. Let the herbs burn out,
then scatter them to the wind. Then quickly (but carefully)
finish filling out and signing the forms. Feel free to save a bit
of the herb mixture to sprinkle on the letter before you send
it. Expect a favorable reply!

Rags to Riches
(or at Least Survival) Spell

Poverty is only romantic if it is happening to a character in a musical, right? And that is only when a rich hero is coming! When you are at the end of a dwindling bank account, for whatever reason, sometimes all you can pin your hopes to is a little magic. This is an old spell that actually worked for me. My act of will involved my last three hundred dollars and a mink stole. But this kind of spell requires total belief! If you've got what it takes and your need is great enough, go for it!

This spell hinges on what is called an act of will—that is, a leap of faith and a strong belief that the universe will care for you! Also, you must *really* need the money.

YOU WILL NEED
+ A significant percentage of what's left of your pitiful savings
+ A lot of guts!

THE SPELL
Take the cash out of the bank and hold it, saying:

NOTHING TO LOSE
TRUSTING TRUE WILL
I OPEN MY ARMS
SO MAY THEY FILL
OM!

Now, go out with a clear mind and spend it all on something completely absurd that you happen to desire. Any whim or silly notion is fine, as long as you do so with complete faith that a new job or whatever you need is right around the corner. *Believe!* Buying something for a loved one is even better. Completely enjoy your new purchase or pleasure.

Enjoy it completely and with no fear!

If you do this with complete confidence, within a day or two, so it is said, something will happen to completely turn around your financial reality—a leap of faith indeed! Geronimo!

STEADY MONEY SPELL

3/27/0~
to 4/2/0~ ✓

What do most people really want—to win the lottery? Yeah,
that would be fine, but don't most of us regular types just
want to make it every month, maybe with enough left over for
vices, fun, and a little savings? We want *regular* paychecks or
royalties or whatever! This folksy little spell has been around
for a while and seems to meet the need even today!

YOU WILL NEED
+ A garden plot, planter, or big planting pot
+ Seven tulip bulbs
+ Seven brand-new pennies

THE SPELL
The best day to do this is on the spring equinox, but any full
moon in the early spring will do.

Dig seven holes in a flower bed in front of your home or in a
planter or a pot. Take the bulbs and pennies there at twilight
and hold them, saying:

> Hertha, heed this my prayer
> Bring each week prosperity
> As you grow each flower
> With me gold shower
> Hear me now, so shall it be!

Plant in each hole a coin and then a bulb, repeating each time:

> Hertha, hertha, heed my prayer

Water each of them, saying in turn:

> Prosperity come a monday
> Prosperity come a tuesday
> Prosperity come a wednesday

PROSPERITY COME A THURSDAY
PROSPERITY COME A FRIDAY
PROSPERITY COME A SATURDAY
PROSPERITY COME A SUNDAY

Then water all the bulbs.

Repeat this chant and this watering for one week straight, and
your weekly prosperity will be firmly implanted! Watch for
amazing things when the tulips bloom!

Inner Wealth Spell

You've got so much—anyway, that is how it looks. You know that most of the world is much poorer than you and you are lucky to be able to have the life you do, but inside you feel bankrupt. How does one create inner prosperity and joy for oneself? The wisdom of developing inner wealth bestows the knowledge that you can survive anything financial. It really is what is important in life. Money cannot buy happiness, but mixed with magic, it can help!

You Will Need
+ A green helium-filled balloon tied to a piece of ribbon
+ A five-dollar bill and a purple felt-tip pen

The Spell

At midday on a Saturday go out to a large open space. I use a
pasture when I am out of the city. When I am in the city, I use
a park or a baseball field. Hold on to the balloon, and say:

Eurus! Notus!
Money comes and money goes
Inner wealth is mine to hold
No matter where the four winds blow
Inner wealth is my inner gold.

Write a note on the five-dollar bill about what you want to
release from your life, like fears of financial insecurity, greed,
or becoming fixated on material things. Then hold open your
palms, lift your face up to the sky, and say:

Zephyrus! Boreas!
Inner wealth is mine to hold
No matter where the four winds blow

Inner wealth is always free
What I let go of
Returns to me!

Feel the solid ground beneath your feet. Attach the note to
the balloon string and let it go, let go, *let go!* As the balloon
soars away, so will your blues! Now go out and donate time or
money to others less fortunate than you!

What a Deal Spell

Need to find just the right knickknack to make your collection complete? Looking for that rare item you *must* have? Others find little nuggets and pearls of treasure at flea markets. It's about time that you too started to get what you are looking for! This spell will fine-tune your bargain-hunting skills and help you find just what you need!

You Will Need
+ A small (five inches long or so) forked stick that you have found and peeled the bark off of
+ A little pure olive oil

THE SPELL

Yes, this is based on dowsing a bit, and seems to work!
On or near a full moon, take your little forked stick and rub
the olive oil into it, saying:

FIND FIND
WHAT IS IN MY MIND
STAFF OF TRUTH LET ME SEE
WHAT I SEEK
BRING IT TO ME!
REVALATO!

Keep this on your person for three days. Then it is ready for use.

Simply do this: When you are at a flea market, antique shop,
specialty shop, or wherever you are hunting for that special
item, take the stick out of your pocket, hold the forked end in
your palm, and point the stick (subtly!) away from you. Close
your eyes and imagine exactly what you want while turning

slowly in a circle clockwise. If you are really focusing, you will feel a slight pull at some point. Follow this pull and you will find what you seek. It takes a bit of practice, but success will be yours!

Happy hunting!

Tax Break Spell

Death and taxes, right? The only sure things, though I think magic is somewhere right behind them! When the tax man cometh, no amount of whining is going to change it. Even though we can't stop the government from taking our money, we *can* try to bend the universe a bit so that it isn't as bad as it could be. That is what this little spell is all about.

You Will Need
+ A small plate
+ Prepared tax documents or the envelope in which you'll send them
+ A small strip of orange paper
+ A red pen
+ Matches

The Spell

On a night when the moon is almost black (waning), place the
plate on top of the prepared tax documents or envelope.

Place the orange paper on the plate, and use the red pen to
draw these runes on the strip, saying as you do so:

FEHU
WEALTH OF MINE
HELP ME HOLD

KENAZ
NEEDFIRE PROTECT ME
FROM THIEF SO BOLD

GEBO
KEEP MY WEALTH SAFE
HELP KEEP MY GOLD!

VALKNUTR MAKE IT SO!

Burn the paper completely and clap three times. Put a dab of
the ash on the document or envelope and toss the rest of the
ashes out the window. Come refund time, you should be
pleasantly surprised!

Magic Penny-Toss Spell

I promise I'm not making this up. This is a spell my grandpa
taught me to use when we needed a small chunk of cash
(under a thousand dollars) for an emergency, like when the
fridge died. As I mentioned in the introduction, I taught this
spell to an audience of a TV show I was appearing on and the
next week they received calls from people who did it and won
money, I kid you not! Now, honey, I know *I'm* good, but if this
can work for those gals, it can work for you!

You Will Need
+ Five new pennies
+ A good throwing arm

Okay, now you've got to *need* this quick cash, right? Keep that
focused in your mind.

First, clean the house or apartment.
Then, stand in the open doorway of your home, facing out.
Take the pennies in your right hand and say:

MONEY COME IN
MONEY GO OUT
MONEY COME IN
PLEASE STAY IN THIS HOUSE!

Then toss the pennies over your shoulder into the home
without looking.

Now, here's the hard part. You have to leave those pennies
where they fall for at least one week! If you touch them or
move them, you'll break the spell. If you let them be,
something good is gonna happen to you real soon!

CARD SPELLS FOR Money Magic

Some kids grow up playing with dolls or toy soldiers. I was lucky enough to grow up playing with fortune-telling! My grandparents insisted on teaching me this stuff, and what I learned first and best was the magic of playing cards. To you, they indicate a poker game or bridge, but to me, they are pure magic! Some of the first spells I learned were card spells. Here are a couple I began using when I was just a kid—and they work as well now as they did then!

CARD SPELL One:

You Will Need
+ A little salt
+ A new pack of cards, never before opened
+ Matches

+ A green candle
+ A small green piece of paper
+ A small plate

(You may also want to use some of the other items mentioned below, but they are not necessary)

Now, the most powerful money magic card is the ace of diamonds. This card has many things connected with it:

Meaning: money, money, and more money!
Scent, incense, or oil: jasmine.
Candle: dark green
Stone: jade

THE ACE OF DIAMONDS:
+ Brings great fortune! Use it in a spell before you sell to get the best price.
+ Can be used to get a giant windfall or to increase your finances in a positive manner.

♦ Increases the luck of those who use it in a spell.
♦ Increases the ability to think creatively when coming up
with that million-dollar idea.
♦ Brings great fortune to those who share it wisely.
♦ Is a great card to use in a spell to bring more joy
and happiness to your life.
♦ Wonderful to use in a spell to help friends.

There are lots of ways to use it to help with money magic.
Simply having it displayed when you do any money spell will
help quite a bit. You can carry it with you to a job interview or
tape it to the mirror when doing "I'm gonna get rich"
affirmations in the morning!

THE SPELL

Do this spell any time you like. Sprinkle salt about the area.
Take out the ace of diamonds. Then light the candle and
meditate on what you want to happen. Write your desire on

the paper and place it on the plate. Clap your hands three times and say these words, or something like them:

CARD OF POWER, CARD OF MEANING
LET ME GIVE YOU NOW THIS GREETING
I HAVE A DESIRE THAT I KNOW IS TRUE
HERE IS MY REQUEST THAT I GIVE TO YOU.
(Say out loud what you want)
CARD OF POWER—MAKE IT TRUE!

Burn the paper. Clap your hands three times and then blow out the candle and say the following:

CARD OF WILL, CARD OF POWER
THANK YOU FOR GRANTING MY DESIRE
FOR HELPING ME DO WHAT I WILL DO
NOW MY WISH WILL COME TRUE!

Leave everything just the way it is!

You should burn the candle like this each night for one week until the spell is finished. Do not remove any of the objects for one week. At the end of the seventh day, let the candle burn down completely. Your wish should materialize very soon!

CARD SPELL TWO: 3/23/02 to 3/29/02

Okay, so now you know how to do a basic card spell! There are many combinations you can use and you can also cross two cards to create a more specific spell. Card spells are endless! But here are a couple of ideas you can use now:

Do this spell just like Card Spell One, but add these other cards for specific money magic goals. To get:

Money from/for work: Place the ace of diamonds on top of the ace of clubs

Money from/for love: Place the ace of diamonds
on top of the ace of hearts
Money to overcome a big problem: Place the ace of
diamonds on top of the ace of spades

To get money from/for a specific person: Place the ace of
diamonds on top of a face card representing that person.
(This is up to you, though generally Kings are mature men,
Queens mature women, and Jacks young men or women,
or boys or girls.)

For example, if I want my young blond niece to get money
for her college classes, I might do a spell with the ace of
diamonds covering the jack of hearts.

Then I would send her those cards after the spell was
finished to keep as good luck charms!

Now you know what it *really* means when someone says,
"It was in the cards!"

The Going for the Gold Spell

You have a dream . . . a goal . . . a mountain to climb . . . a river to ford! Something you, darn it, *want!* Maybe it is a promotion, a raise, a chunk of cash for a trip, a house or a car . . . it is material and you really, really want it and are working toward getting it. To get it requires luck and money! Wanna reach that financial/material object of desire? Then do this spell. But be sure you really are dedicated before you do!

You Will Need
+ A plate (earthenware is best, no metal!)
+ Two small candles (one green, one white)
+ A brand-new needle
+ Matches

THE SPELL

On the night of the quarter moon (waxing) set up the plate in
front of you while facing north. Place the green candle on the
left side of the plate, the white one on the right. Hold the
needle in your hand and make a clockwise circle with it about
the plate, saying:

HERE I conjure
SELF and GOAL
BOTH BE joined
In my soul!
ABRAHADABRA!

With the needle, scratch your secret or personal name on the
white candle. Whisper the name and put down the candle.
Use the pin to write your goal on the green candle, then
whisper this too. Light both candles and place the needle
between them, saying:

THIS I WILL
THIS I MAKE
THAT MY GOAL
MY SELF SHALL TAKE!
ABRAHADABRA!

Let them burn for a little while, then blow them out.
Then move the candles a little bit closer together.

Repeat the lighting of the candles and the actions in this
fashion every night for one week, making sure that you don't
burn the candles down too fast!
On the seventh night, the night of the full moon, the candles
should be almost finished and together.

Thrust the needle through both candles, pinning them
together, and say:

TOGETHER JOINED
TOGETHER ONE!
AS THE UNION
OF MOON AND SUN!
ABRAHADABRA!

Light both candles at once and let them
burn down completely.

You should gain your desire soon, though you'll still have to
work for it! If you try sometimes, you just might find
you get what you need!

Prosperity Wash Over Me Spell

It is truly amazing how similar people from every country and culture are. Whether in Egypt, India, Canada, or wherever, we all like prosperity and the comforts a good life can bring us. It is also amazing that in so many different places, I've seen variants of this spell, the same one my grandmother taught me, though I've spiced it up a bit! It is called a "wash" and is simply a kind of cleaning spell. The idea is to clean out all the bad mojo and wash the floors, counters, and so on with good mojo-makin' magic. It will soon be featured in *Better Homes & Spells* . . . ha!

You Will Need
+ Water
+ Some salt
+ Some vinegar

- A bucket and new cleaning things, mop and cloth,
for example
- A cooking pot
- Some catnip (fresh is best)

THE SPELL

On a Sunday, open all your doors and windows if you can,
then clean house with warm water mixed with salt and
vinegar. Clean as well as you can, making sure you are also
putting things away and so on. All the time you are
doing this, mutter:

Out tout
Throughout and about
All good come in
All evil go out!

Thoroughly clean your mop and cloths.

Put a pot of water on the stove and bring it to a boil. Into it
toss a handful of catnip, saying the previous verse once again,
then take the pot off the stove.

After a little time, pour a bit of this catnip tea into
a teacup and much of the rest into a clean bucket.
The herbs should have settled, so it should be mostly
free of leaves.

Sip the catnip tea (it won't hurt you!) and then
wash the whole house with the tea in the bucket,
saying over and over again:

FILL THIS HOME WITH JOY AND MIRTH
FILL THIS HOME WITH TREASURES OF EARTH
FILL THIS HOME WITH RICHES GALORE
FILL THIS HOME WITH ALL I ADORE

When done, pour the excess tea/water about the outside of
the home and repeat this last verse one more time. Bury
the finished herbs from the pot and thank the Earth
(and your lucky stars!) for all the great things that
are gonna come your way!

01/28/02

PROSPERITY BLESSINGS OF THE EIGHT TRIGRAMS

The eight trigrams are some of the oldest magical symbols in the world. Coming from ancient China, they represent the eight primal powers of the universe (for more on the trigrams, read any translation of the *I Ching*). Each of these primal powers can be called upon to help you.

It is traditional to draw the trigram of the power you wish to call (on a piece of paper or wood) and then read the appropriate spell. After that, keep this charm in your house or workplace, or give it as a gift.

There are wealth spells for each of the eight primal trigram symbols.

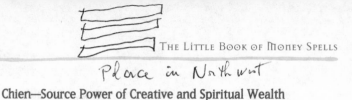

Place in Northwest

Chien—Source Power of Creative and Spiritual Wealth

WEALTH OF HEAVEN
DRAGON POWER OF THE CREATIVE
SOURCE OF ALL SPIRIT-FILLING ALL
WORK AND PLAY, LOVE AND WILL
RICHES AND JOY WITHIN AND WITHOUT
CHIEN! GIFT OF HEAVEN, ABIDE HERE!

Place in southeast

Suun—The Power of Wind-Blown Healing Wealth

WINDS OF WEALTH, SWIRL
BRILLIANT DRAGON OF AIR BRING WEALTH
LIGHTNESS OF BEING, SPIRIT OF HEALING
FILL EVERY BREATH, EVERY STEP, EVERY ACTION
PENETRATING POWER OF PROSPERITY
SUUN! COSMIC BREATH, INSPIRE!

143

Li—The Power of Fiery and Ambitious Wealth

FLASHING FIERY RICHES
FLAMING DRAGON OF PASSION
GIFTS OF GOLD AND GLORY
WEALTH OF AMBITION, GREAT WORKS, AND JEWELS
FLY INTO OUR HANDS, HOUSE, AND WORKPLACE
ENFLAME OUR TRUE WILL TO GREATNESS
LI! BLESSING OF SUN-FIRE, EMBRACE US!

Place in NE

Ken—The Power of the Mountain: ✓
Solid, Stable, and Balanced Wealth

WEALTH OF DEEP MOUNTAINS
DRAGON OF PEAKS AND PASSES, STILLNESS
AND BALANCE
EARTH US IN THE OLD WEALTH
POWER OF MINES AND MOUNTAIN OF RICHES
PROSPEROUS STABILITY, WEALTH, AND WORLDLY POWER
KEN! MOUNTAIN OF PROSPERITY, MAY WE REST
UPON YOU!

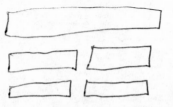

145

✓

Place in the We[...]

Tui—Power of the Lake:
Wealth of Pleasure, Happiness, and Fun

WEALTH OF PLEASURE AND HAPPY FUN, GROW HERE
BLUE DRAGON OF THE LAKE OF HAPPINESS, ARISE
EASY WEALTH, SPENT AND GIVEN FREELY
GOOD-TIME RICHES, POUR AS WATER INTO MY
CUPPED HANDS
LET ME DRINK OF WEALTH AND SATISFACTION,
FRIENDSHIP AND FUN
TUI! RIPPLES OF PROSPERITY, FLOW!

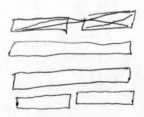

Kan—Power of Rain and Dark Prosperity:
Protection and Hidden Wealth

Secret wealth of protection, manifest
Dark dragon of inner silences and overcoming
Remove all obstacles to prosperity
Bring psychic wealth and clear vision
Open the inner eye to reveal hidden riches
Kan! prosperity in hard times, protect
and reveal!

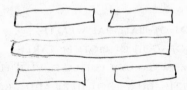

Chen—Power of Lightning-Strike: Sudden Prosperity

Lightning, thunder—sudden wealth!
Sparkling dragon of power, descend!
In a flash fill our arms with unexpected riches!
Shocking, bold path of prosperity
Open new ways, new sights, new veins of gold!
Chen! arousing electric prosperity, strike!

Place in
Southwest

Kun—Power of the Fruits of the Earth, General Wealth, and Wish Fulfillment

Root of material wealth
Green dragon of mother earth
Fulfill desires as a garden is filled with flowers
Tree of wealth, take root here and grow!
Valley spirit, give us ten thousand things!
Kun! earth spirit, grant all wishes!